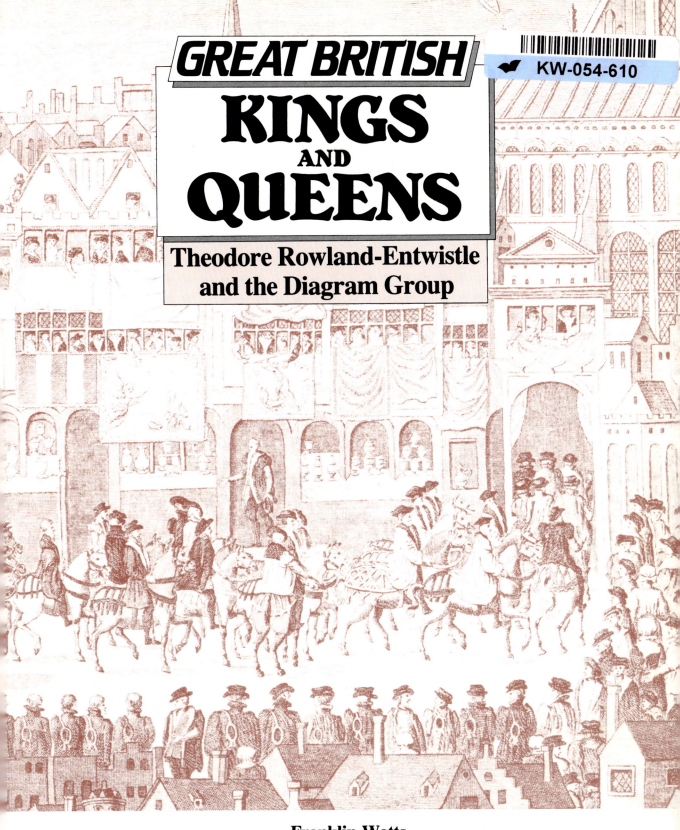

GREAT BRITISH

KINGS
AND
QUEENS

Theodore Rowland-Entwistle
and the Diagram Group

Franklin Watts
London New York Sydney Toronto

Queen Elizabeth II meeting schoolchildren during her visit to the West Indies in 1983

Acknowledgements
Picture research: IKON
Cover: Camera Press
BBC Hulton Picture Library: 7, 8
British Museum: 22, 23
Courtauld Institute: 19
Crown Copyright: 30
Dean and Chapter of Westminster: 28
Illustrated London News: 34–35
Arthur Lockwood: 30
Mansell Collection: 17, 21, 24, 34–35
National Portrait Gallery: 30

KINGS AND QUEENS   ARCHITECTS

BOUDICA

EDWARD THE CONFESSOR

WILLIAM THE CONQUEROR

JONES

WREN

HAWKSMOOR

RICHARD I

EDWAR

ADAM

NASH

HENRY VII

HENRY

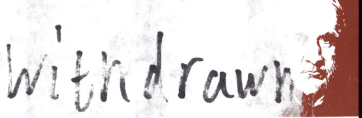

withdrawn

SCOTT

SHAW

JAMES VI AND I

CHARLES I

MACKINTOSH

LUTYENS

GEORGE III

VICTORIA

ELIZABETH II

DREW

STIRLING

FOSTER

The Coronation procession of Edward VI

Contents

© Diagram Visual Information Ltd 1986

First published in Great Britain 1986 by
Franklin Watts Ltd
12a Golden Square
London W1

Printed in Singapore

ISBN 0 86313 367 3

When they lived

4

1215 Magna
Carta signed

1314 Battle of
Bannockburn

1492 Columbus
discovered West Indies

| 1000 | 1100 | 1200 | 1300 | 1400 |

Edward the Confessor
1002–1066

William the Conqueror
1028–1087

Richard I
1157–1199

Edward I
1239–1307

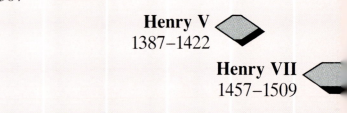

Henry V
1387–1422

Henry VII
1457–1509

| 1000 | 1100 | 1200 | 1300 | 1400 |

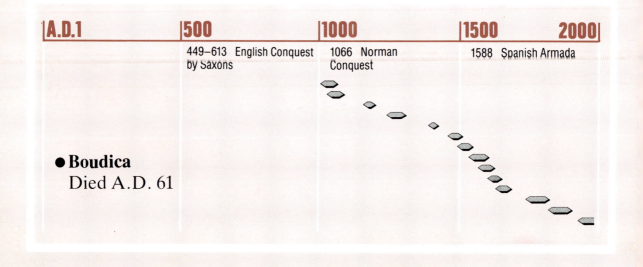

| A.D.1 | 500 | 1000 | 1500 | 2000 |

449–613 English Conquest
by Saxons

1066 Norman
Conquest

1588 Spanish Armada

● **Boudica**
Died A.D. 61

1558–1603 Queen
Elizabeth I reigned

1642–1651 English
Civil War

1746 Bonnie Prince
Charlie defeated at Culloden

1879 Zulu War

1939–1945
Second World War

|500 **|1600** **|1700** **|1800** **|1900** **|2000**

Henry VIII
1491–1547

Elizabeth I
1533–1603

James VI and I
1566–1625

Charles I
1600–1649

Charles II
1630–1685

George III
1738–1820

Victoria
1819–1901

Elizabeth II
1926–

500 **1600** **1700** **1800** **1900** **2000**

Boudica

Roman tombstone mutilated by Boudica's followers

Boudica was queen of the Iceni, a tribe of Celtic Britons that lived among the fens of what is now Norfolk at the time of the Roman conquest of Britain. She became their ruler when her husband Prasutagus died.

Prasutagus left his personal property jointly to his two daughters and the Roman emperor, Nero, hoping this move would safeguard his family and kingdom. The Romans, however, interpreted the king's will as giving the whole kingdom to them, and soldiers and slaves began looting it.

Boudica, a tall, fiery-tempered woman, with a harsh voice and long red hair, protested at the Romans' conduct. To teach her a lesson the Romans stripped her naked and flogged her, and assaulted her two daughters. Boudica vowed revenge. She led the Iceni to revolt, supported by several neighbouring tribes. The rebellion was well timed, because the governor of Britain, Suetonius Paulinus, was fighting a campaign in Wales.

Boudica and her army marched on Camulodunum (now Colchester), where there was a large colony of Roman ex-soldiers. The Iceni burned the city and killed every Roman and pro-Roman Briton in it. The Britons then moved on to London and Verulamium (modern St Albans) and destroyed them too. Altogether they slaughtered more than 70,000 men, women, and children.

Meanwhile Suetonius gathered an army of 10,000 trained legionaries. He lay in wait for the Britons, probably on the main Roman road between the modern towns of Nuneaton and Tamworth. Boudica led her much larger army of Britons to the attack. It was a motley mob of half-naked men followed by wagons carrying women and children eager to see the fun. It was no match for the well-disciplined and heavily armed Romans. Thousands of Britons were killed and the rest fled. Boudica escaped, but killed herself soon after.

The skull of a Londoner killed by Boudica's followers

**'The Warrior Patriot Queen',
Boudica's statue in London**

Edward the Confessor

The Great Seal of Edward the Confessor

Edward the Confessor at a banquet

Edward was the son of King Ethelred II the Redeless (badly-advised). His mother, Emma, was the daughter of Duke Richard of Normandy. As a boy Edward was brought up in Normandy, while England was under the rule of the Danish king Cnut and his two sons. When Ethelred died Emma married Cnut. Their son Harthacnut, who became king in 1040, invited his older half-brother Edward to England and accepted him as his heir. Harthacnut died of drink at the age of 25 and Edward became king.

Edward was peace-loving, very pious and more Norman than Saxon in his ways. He invited some of his Norman friends to England and gave them posts at court, but these Normans had little power. England was controlled by Saxon earls, led by Earl Godwine.

In 1045 the king married Godwine's daughter Editha, but he had no love for his father-in-law or for Editha's brothers, Swein, Harold, Tostig and Gyrth. In 1051 Godwine refused to punish the people of Dover, who had brawled with some

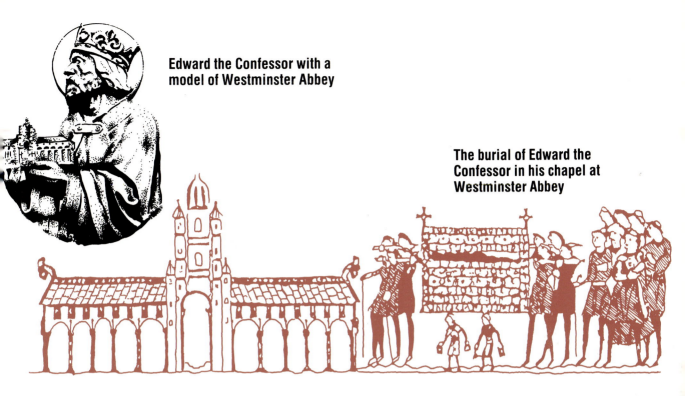

Edward the Confessor with a model of Westminster Abbey

The burial of Edward the Confessor in his chapel at Westminster Abbey

Norman visitors. With the support of two other earls, Leofric of Mercia and Siward of Northumbria, Edward promptly banished Godwine and his sons, and sent Editha to live in a convent. He invited more Normans to England, and his cousin Duke William of Normandy came on a state visit. It is said that Edward, who had no children, promised to make William heir to the English throne.

Two years later Godwine and his family returned to England with a large army, and forced Edward to restore them - and Queen Editha - to favour. Godwine once more became the real ruler of the country, and when he died his son Harold took charge of affairs.

For the rest of his reign Edward was able to turn most of his attention to religion, which earned him the name of 'the Confessor'. His last act was the building of Westminster Abbey, which was completed just in time for him to be buried there in 1066. He was canonised (declared a saint) in 1161.

Edward the Confessor's portrait on the Bayeux Tapestry

William the Conqueror

Scenes from the life of William I from the Bayeux Tapestry

The Great Seal of William I

William I, who by seizing England has gone down in history as 'the Conqueror', was a strong, ruthless yet wise ruler and the best general of his time. He was the illegitimate, and only, son of Robert, Duke of Normandy. He succeeded his father as duke at the age of seven. Guardians ruled his duchy while he was a child, but from the age of 15 he took charge, and over the next few years fought a series of campaigns to subdue his turbulent barons.

England at that time was ruled by the Saxon king Edward the Confessor, who had no children to succeed him. William always claimed that Edward had promised him the throne. The other main candidate for the throne was Earl Harold Godwinesson, a powerful Saxon noble who virtually ruled England in Edward's name.

When Edward died the Saxon English chose Harold as king. Nine months later William and an army of adventurers recruited from all over

Europe landed at Pevensey, in Sussex. They defeated and killed Harold at the Battle of Hastings. The English were left without a leader, and William quickly made himself master of England.

William rewarded his followers with lands in England, wrested from the Saxons. He also introduced what historians call the feudal system into England. Under this system, the most important nobles held their lands directly from the king, and granted some of those lands to lesser lords. William's rule was stern, but fair. He kept such good order in the land that, as a Saxon monk wrote in the *Anglo-Saxon Chronicle,* a history of the times, 'a man could travel through the country with a bosom full of gold unmolested.'

Among William's last acts was to order a complete survey of England so that he knew what taxes he could impose. It still survives, and is known as the *Domesday Book.*

1028
Born in Falaise, Normandy
1035
Became Duke of Normandy
1066
Defeated Harold at the Battle of Hastings
Crowned King of England in Westminster Abbey
1068
Returned to England from Normandy to crush revolts
1071
English rebellion finally quelled
1083
Land survey ordered, which resulted in the *Domesday Book* (1085-86)
1087
War in France. William fatally injured
Died 9th September in Rouen, France
Buried at Caen

Richard I

The Great Seal of Richard I

1157
Born 8th September in Oxford
1172
Created Duke of Aquitaine
1189
Became King of England and set out on crusade
1190
Married Berengaria of Navarre
1191
Captured Acre
1192
Sailed for England; captured by Duke Leopold of Austria
1193
Handed over to German emperor Henry VI
1194
Ransomed and returned briefly to England
1199
Fatally wounded at siege of Castle of Châlus; died 6th April

Richard I was one of the most glamorous and popular kings of England, and one of the most useless to his country. He reigned for ten years, and spent only six months in England. He was a poet and musician, but his courage and skill as a warrior earned him the nickname of 'the Lion-Heart'. He was tall and red-haired, quick-tempered yet chivalrous.

Richard was the third son of Henry II. At the age of 11 he was made Duke of Aquitaine, his mother's duchy, then part of Henry's vast lands in France.

When Henry II died in 1189, Richard, as the eldest surviving son, succeeded him. He at once forgave and rewarded all those barons who had opposed his rebellions and been loyal to his father. He had only one thought: to go on crusade to the Holy Land (Palestine) to recapture Jerusalem from the Saracens (the Arab Muslims).

A few weeks after his coronation Richard set out on the crusade. The English Crusaders joined

Richard I at the battle of Azotus

forces with a French army led by its king, Philip II, and Crusaders from Austria and Germany. In the fighting Richard was the outstanding warrior, capturing the city of Acre and twice almost freeing Jerusalem. However, there were many quarrels among the Crusaders, and in 1192 Richard decided to make peace with the Saracens and return to England, where his brother John was trying to seize the throne. On the way he was captured by Duke Leopold of Austria, and handed over to the German emperor, Henry VI. Henry eventually released him on payment of a huge ransom.

Richard returned to England, where he forgave the rebellious John. Within a few weeks he set out to defend his French lands, which were being attacked by Philip II. The campaign lasted five years. It ended only when Richard was fatally wounded by a crossbow bolt while besieging the castle of Châlus in a petty quarrel over treasure-trove.

Richard I fighting a lion

The tombs of Richard I and his mother, Eleanor of Aquitaine

Edward I

Edward I earned three nicknames: 'Longshanks' because of his long legs; 'The Hammer of the Scots' as a result of his campaigns against Scotland; and 'The Lawgiver' in view of his reforms of English laws.

When Edward came to the throne at the age of 33, he had already had a great deal of experience in fighting and politics, trying to sort out the chaotic affairs of his incompetent father, Henry III. When Henry died in 1272, Edward was away on the Sixth Crusade. He had left reliable and capable men in charge of the kingdom, and did not trouble to return home for nearly two years.

After his coronation Edward launched a campaign against the Welsh, who were raiding the border districts of England. The Welsh agreed to submit, but later rebelled, so Edward conquered Wales, and incorporated it as part of England. He gave the title Prince of Wales to his baby son, Edward.

Having subdued Wales, Edward turned his eyes on Scotland, of which he claimed to be overlord. Alexander III of Scotland died, leaving as queen a two-year-old granddaughter, Margaret of Norway. Edward negotiated a marriage between Margaret and his heir, the young Prince of Wales, but Margaret died at the age of seven, leaving two main claimants to the Scottish throne, Robert Bruce and John Balliol. They asked Edward to decide who had the better claim.

Edward chose Balliol, who acknowledged Edward as his overlord, but in 1295 Balliol rebelled, and Edward marched into Scotland and seized power. The Scots were not easily crushed. Edward put down a rebellion by a Scottish knight,

The Great Seal of Edward I

Edward I and his parliament

The Scottish coronation stone set into the throne in Westminster Abbey

Sir William Wallace, in 1297, but in 1306 Robert Bruce had himself crowned King of Scots. Edward was marching north to subdue this rebellion when he died near Carlisle.

Edward's laws were aimed at preventing the Church from acquiring too much property, making sure that landowners left their property to their eldest sons, and reorganising the national militia. Edward held regular parliaments, and his 'Model Parliament' of 1295 included representatives of towns and counties as well as the barons and Church leaders.

1239
Born 17th June at Westminster Palace
1254
Married Eleanor of Castile
1272
Proclaimed King
1274
Crowned at Westminster
1277-1284
Conquered Wales and made it part of England
1290
Death of Queen Eleanor
1292
Chose Balliol as King of Scots
1295
'Model Parliament'
1297-1298
Wallace led Scots revolt
1299
Married Margaret of France
1306
Bruce crowned King of Scots
1307
Died in Burgh-on-Sands, Cumbria

The Great Seal of Henry V

The thanksgiving service on the field of Agincourt

Henry V

By the time Henry V became king at the age of 26 he was already a seasoned warrior, who had fought a long civil war against the Welsh. He had also helped to administer the country during the last years of his ailing father, Henry IV.

The young king was a pious man. He was ambitious for more military glory, and he revived the claim of his great-grandfather, Edward III, to the throne of France in the belief that right and God were on his side. The English, tired of civil wars and other internal quarrels, supported him whole-heartedly.

Two years after Henry ascended the throne he led an army of 10,000 men to France. They landed at the mouth of the River Seine, where they captured the town of Harfleur. Illness struck down several thousand of his soldiers, and Henry decided to march with fewer than 6,000 men to Calais, to take ship for home.

The French *dauphin* (crown prince) barred his way, with an army nearly 20,000 strong. Henry refused to retreat. One of his generals wished for more men, but Henry replied: 'Wot you not that the Lord with these few can overthrow the pride of the French?' When the two armies met near the village of Agincourt, Henry and his archers won an overwhelming victory.

It took Henry a long and costly campaign, lasting from 1417 to 1420, before he could finally defeat the French. By a treaty the French king, Charles VI, recognised Henry as his heir, and Henry married Charles' daughter, Catherine. Two months before Charles' death Henry himself died, from an illness contracted while fighting. He left as king a baby son, Henry VI, just nine months old.

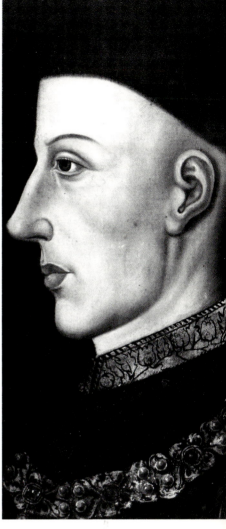

1387
Born 16th September in Monmouth, Gwent
1403-1408
War against Welsh rebels
1413
Became king
1415
Victories at Harfleur and Agincourt
1417-1420
Second French campaign
1420
Became heir to French throne, married Catherine
1422
Died 31st August

Henry V's helmet, shield and saddle

Henry VII

Henry VII united England after the Wars of the Roses, the civil wars between the opposing royal families of York and Lancaster who had been fighting for the crown for 30 years from 1455 to 1485. Henry was the last surviving male of the House of Lancaster, to which his mother belonged. His father was Edmund Tudor, Earl of Richmond.

Henry won the crown by defeating and killing his Yorkist rival, King Richard III, in battle at Bosworth Field in Leicestershire. He then married Richard's niece, Elizabeth of York, uniting the two families.

There were still several Yorkist claimants to the throne. Henry had to subdue rebellions on behalf of them, as well as two false claimants, Lambert Simnel and Perkin Warbeck. The Wars of the Roses had killed many of the old nobility and Henry created new nobles, loyal to himself. Henry

The Great Seal of Henry VII

Henry VII giving the indenture for the foundation of the King's Chapel in Westminster Abbey

realised the necessity of having money, and set himself to amass a fortune. He was helped by his Lord Chancellor, Cardinal John Morton, who levied forced loans from rich men. The wealthy were made to contribute on the grounds that they could obviously afford it, and those who lived economically were told they must have savings. This two-pronged argument was known as 'Morton's Fork'.

Having acquired wealth, Henry was careful not to spend it, especially on war. When he did become involved in a war with France, he allowed the French to pay him to make peace. When he did spend, it was on the chapel he added to Westminster Abbey.

Henry VII combined the skills of a businessman with the craft of a diplomat, and he left the country to his son, Henry VIII, at peace and with a full treasury.

1457
Born 28th January at Pembroke Castle, Wales
1471-1485
In exile in Brittany
1485
Defeated Richard III at Battle of Bosworth Field, became king 1486
1486
Married Elizabeth of York
1487
Crushed rebellion led by pretender Lambert Simnel
1491
Capture of pretender Perkin Warbeck
1499
Execution of Warbeck
1503
Daughter Margaret married James IV of Scotland
1509
Died 21st April in Richmond, Surrey

Henry VII's effigy in Westminster Abbey

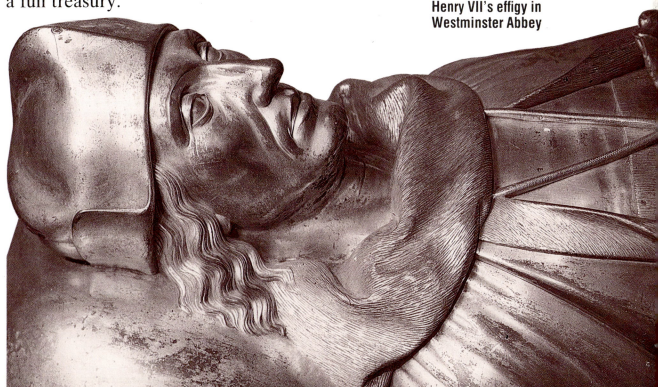

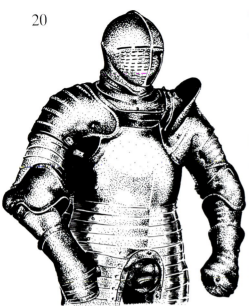

Henry VIII's armour

1491
Born 28th June in Greenwich
1509
Became king; married Catherine of Aragon
1533
Divorced Catherine and married Anne Boleyn
1534
Henry declared head of the Church of England
1536
Anne Boleyn beheaded. Married Jane Seymour
1536-1540
Dissolution of monasteries
1537
Jane died after giving birth to a son
1540
Married Anne of Cleves, divorced her and married Catherine Howard
1542
Catherine Howard beheaded
1543
Married Catherine Parr
1547
Died 28th January in London

Henry VIII

Henry was born in Greenwich in 1491, the second son of Henry VII and Elizabeth of York. In 1509 he succeeded his father to a peaceful country with a full treasury. As a younger son Henry had been destined for the church, but when his older brother Arthur died, Henry became king. He decided to marry his brother's widow, a Spanish princess, Catherine of Aragon, to maintain a political alliance with Spain.

A sovereign of exceptional energy and personality, he was ruthless to all who opposed him. A succession of brilliant ministers - Wolsey, Sir Thomas More, Thomas Cromwell - aided him in ruling his kingdom with absolute power in matters of religion and government. He became head of the Church of England having broken with the Church of Rome over the Pope's refusal to grant him a divorce. He proceeded to dissolve the monasteries and seized their lands.

Henry married six times: Catherine of Aragon, mother of Mary I, he divorced; Anne Boleyn, mother of Elizabeth I, he had beheaded; Jane Seymour, mother of Edward VI, died in childbirth; Anne of Cleves, he divorced; Catherine Howard, he had beheaded for adultery; and Catherine Parr outlived him.

Henry was a scholar, a linguist, a musician and an athlete as a young man. After he had invaded France early in his reign and beaten the Scots at Flodden Field in 1513, his later policies aimed at peace with Europe and order at home. He built up the English navy to challenge the might of Spain. He steered England through the Reformation without the chaos that accompanied the religious revolutions on the Continent.

Henry VIII's six wives

Jane Seymour

Catherine Howard

Anne Boleyn

Anne of Cleves

Catherine of Aragon

Catherine Parr

Elizabeth I

Silver medal commemorating the defeat of the Spanish Armada

1553
Born 7th September at Greenwich Palace
1536
Her mother, Anne Boleyn, executed for adultery
1547
Death of her father, Henry VIII; accession of Edward VI
1553
Death of Edward, accession of Mary
1558
Became queen on the death of Mary I
1559
Enforced Protestant religion
1568
Mary Queen of Scots flees to England
1587
Execution of Mary Queen of Scots
1588
Spanish armada defeated
1603
Died 24th March at Richmond Palace, Surrey

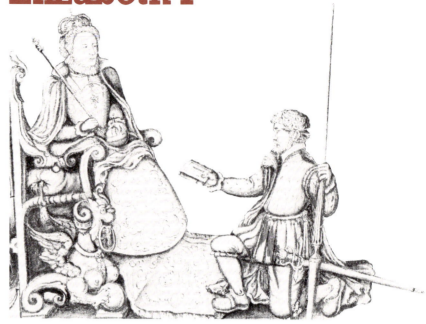

A poet presenting his works to Elizabeth I

Elizabeth I was the daughter of Henry VIII and his second wife, Anne Boleyn. She was declared illegitimate when her mother was executed, but her father had her well educated. She was a fluent scholar in Greek, Latin, French and Italian.

Elizabeth kept clear of political affairs during the brief reigns of her half brother, Edward VI, and her half sister, Mary I. Under Edward the country became fervently Protestant, while Mary tried to return England to the Roman Catholic faith. Most English people greeted the accession in 1558 of Elizabeth, who was known to be Protestant, with relief.

The new queen inherited a dangerous position. The Roman Catholics, supported by Philip II of Spain, were constantly plotting to overthrow her. Her heir, Mary Queen of Scots, was also Roman Catholic but most of her Scots subjects were fiercely Protestant.

Elizabeth was intellectually gifted as well as

Elizabeth I carried in procession by her courtiers

Signature of Elizabeth I

calculating and devious. She surrounded herself with advisers and used the possibility of marriage to her to keep France and Spain anxious.

In 1568 Mary Queen of Scots fled from Scotland after the defeat of her supporters and sought refuge in England. Elizabeth welcomed her, seizing the opportunity to dispose of the threat to her position and imprisoned Mary for 18 years. Eventually Mary was involved in one of the many plots to kill Elizabeth, and reluctantly the queen ordered her cousin's execution.

Although Elizabeth's enemies hated her, most of her subjects loved her. So when Philip of Spain sent an armada, a huge fleet, to invade England, Elizabeth was able to inspire the country to rally to the defence, and the armada was defeated.

During Elizabeth's reign her sailors explored the world. Her glittering court encouraged poets and playwrights such as William Shakespeare, and musicians such as William Byrd and Thomas Tallis.

The tomb of Elizabeth I

James VI and I

James VI and I welcoming home his son Charles I

James was the first monarch to rule over both England and Scotland. He was a member of the Stuart family, which had ruled Scotland since 1371. He became King James VI of Scotland at the age of one when his mother, Mary Queen of Scots, was forced to abdicate. A series of regents ruled Scotland for him until 1583, when he assumed power.

In 1603 he became King James I of England on the death of Elizabeth I. Although he was brought up as a Presbyterian James declared there would be no changes in the Church of England and its bishops, saying 'No bishop, no king.' He opposed the Roman Catholics, who hatched a plot to blow up parliament and James with it. The discovery of this Gunpowder Plot is still celebrated on 5th November.

James believed kings had a divine right to rule, and this view brought him into conflict with

Guy Fawkes and his fellow conspirators

James VI and I sitting for his portrait

England's parliament. James was always asking parliament for money, because inflation was reducing the value of the fixed income he was voted.

The king was a self-opinionated scholar, with a fondness for lecturing his people. He published a number of books of poetry and essays. His contemporary, Henry IV of France, once called him 'The wisest fool in Christendom'.

James' greatest achievement was ordering a new translation of the Bible. This, the *Authorised Version of the Bible,* was completed in 1611, and its beautiful language has made it the most popular translation among English-speaking peoples.

Charles I

Charles I inherited from his father, James VI and I, two things: a belief in the divine right of kings to rule, and a financial crisis. They brought him into conflict with parliament and cost him his life.

The new king was a little man, serious minded, brave and a fine horseman. He had a slight stammer and had suffered from polio in his youth. He was a strictly moral person, faithful to his wife, Henrietta Maria of France, and a good and loving father. However, he neglected the government of his country, which he left to his ministers.

Parliament kept the king short of money to pay for the government of the country, so Charles levied taxes without their consent compelling some of his subjects to 'lend' him money. In 1628 some members of parliament drew up a Petition of Right, demanding that Charles should raise no more forced loans, or levy taxes without parliament's consent. So Charles ruled for 11 years without parliament.

A war with the Scots, whom he tried to force to have bishops in their Church, drove Charles in desperation to ask parliament for help. Parliament demanded the death of Charles' chief minister, the Earl of Strafford, and other demands which Charles refused. Within a few weeks civil war between parliament and king had broken out.

The war raged from 1642 to 1645. Charles became a capable general in those years, but his opponents, and especially their most brilliant general Oliver Cromwell, were too strong for him. He sought shelter with the Scots, who handed him over, a prisoner, to his enemies. He was eventually charged with treason against his people, and after a travesty of a trial he was executed outside his palace of Whitehall.

The Great Seal of Charles I

The death mask of Charles I

1600
Born 19th November at Dunfermline Palace, Fife
1625
Became king; married Henrietta Maria of France
1628
Petition of Right
1629-1640
Ruled without parliament
1641
Execution of Strafford
1642
Civil war broke out
1645
Charles defeated at battles of Marston Moor and Naseby
1646
Scots hand Charles over to English parliament
1649
Tried 19th-27th January and executed 3Oth January

Charles I on trial in the High Court of Justice

Charles II

The wax effigy of Charles II in Westminster Abbey

'The Merry Monarch', as Charles II was known, had the reputation of being pleasure-loving, lazy and cynical. Yet he was one of the shrewdest rulers that Britain ever had.

Charles was just 19 when his father, Charles I, was executed and parliament declared the monarchy abolished. Royalist supporters regarded him as king from that moment, but Charles was in exile in France.

In 1650 he decided to make an effort to win back the throne, and landed in Scotland. There, loyalist Scots crowned him as King of Scotland. Charles led an army into England, but was beaten at the Battle of Worcester and Charles had to flee for his life. After 43 adventurous days Charles landed back in France to begin a further nine years in exile.

The English, tired of republicanism, invited Charles to come back in 1660. With his courtesy and his genial good nature, Charles knew how to damp down hot tempers and extreme views, and heal many of the wounds left by civil war.

Like his father, Charles was given an income that was not enough to pay the running expenses of government, let alone cover his own extravagant tastes. So he turned elsewhere for funds. He signed a secret treaty with his cousin, Louis XIV of France, under which he agreed to declare himself a Roman Catholic, and to support France in a war against the Netherlands. In return Louis gave him a regular yearly allowance.

The Dutch war followed, but Charles, king of a country that was fiercely Protestant, found excuse after excuse for not announcing his Catholicism until he lay dying. In 1678 some fanatics

Entry of Charles II into London

Nell Gwynne

pretended to uncover a 'Popish Plot', which caused so much fuss that Charles' brother James, who was an avowed Roman Catholic and his heir, had to leave England for a time.

Charles was married to a Portuguese princess, Catherine of Branganza, but the couple had no children. The king had 14 illegitimate children by Nell Gwynne and Barbara Villiers, but none of them could inherit the throne. Despite his casual air, the king took an active interest in the affairs of his country, and was a keen scientist.

1630
Born 29th May at St James' Palace, London
1646
Escaped to France
1651
Crowned king in Scotland; defeated at Worcester; escaped to France again
1660
Restored to English throne
1662
Married Catherine of Braganza
1670
Secret treaty with France
1678
'Popish plot' discovered
1685
Died 5th February in Whitehall London

George III

A twopenny piece

1738
Born 4th June in London
1760
Became king
1761
Married Princess Charlotte Sophia of
Mecklenburg-Strelitz
1765
Temporary fit of insanity
1776
American colonies declared their
independence on 4th July
1788-1789
Second fit of insanity
1801
Britain and Ireland formed the United
Kingdom
1810
Became finally insane; son became
Prince Regent
1820
Died 29th January at Windsor Castle

George III was 22 when he succeeded his grandfather, George II, as King of Great Britain, and also Elector of Hanover in Germany. During his 60-year reign Britain turned from an agricultural nation to an industrial one, gained Canada but lost its other American colonies, and fought a long war against the tyranny of Napoleon I of France. Also during the reign Britain and Ireland were amalgamated to form the United Kingdom of Great Britain and Ireland.

George was the third king of the German House of Hanover. He was born and brought up in England, and was fiercely patriotic. He was happiest when living the life of a country squire, and his subjects affectionately nicknamed him 'Farmer George'. He was determined to be a good king, but he was lacking in confidence.

The king's political inexperience led to a series of governments and prime ministers with whom he

George III being disturbed by the entry of his drunken son, the Prince of Wales

disagreed. In 1770 he found a man with whom he could work, Lord North, who was prime minister until 1782. The king and the incompetent North mismanaged relations with Britain's 13 North American colonies, which rebelled and formed the United States of America.

With the much more capable William Pitt, who was prime minister from 1783 to 1801 and again from 1804 to 1806, George was also happy, but he worried about affairs of state so much that he began having fits of madness.

In 1810 he became finally and hopelessly insane. His powers were transferred to his eldest son as Prince Regent. His last years were spent in confinement at Windsor Castle, where from time to time he was well enough to acknowledge his madness. His sole consolation was music.

A cartoon of George III and Queen Charlotte watching the approach of Napoleon

Victoria

The coronation of Victoria

Prince Albert and Victoria in 1851

During Victoria's 63 years on the throne Britain built up a vast empire and underwent a period of enormous technological change, including the invention of the Morse telegraph, the telephone, the electric light and radio.

Victoria was the daughter of George III's third son, the Duke of Kent. She was brought up by her mother in almost complete seclusion at Kensington Palace. She became queen at the age of 18 when her uncle, William IV, died, and at once displayed an unexpected firmness in breaking away from her ambitious and domineering mother. During the early years of her reign she relied on the advice of her first prime minister, Lord Melbourne.

In 1840 Victoria married her cousin, Prince Albert of Saxe-Coburg-Gotha, who received the title of Prince Consort. The prince had a great

Victoria in her Jubilee Year

Victoria in her Coronation Year

deal of influence over the queen, and she became more conscious of her responsibilties and more businesslike. Victoria was devoted to the prince and the couple, together with their nine children, enjoyed a happy family life, preferring Windsor, Balmoral and Osborne House to London. When Prince Albert died in 1861, Victoria plunged herself into deep mourning. She carried out her business and constitutional duties, but rarely appeared in public. Her family connections with many of the European royal houses proved to be useful in political matters. Towards the end of her reign Victoria was content to leave affairs of state to politicians such as Disraeli, but was flattered when she was given the title of Empress of India. Her difficult relationship with her capable but pleasure-loving son (later Edward VII) resulted in his exclusion from political duties.

1819
Born 24th May at Kensington Palace
1837
Became queen
1840
Married Prince Albert of Saxe-Coburg-Gotha
1851
Great Exhibition held in Hyde Park
1854-56
The Crimean War
1861
Death of Prince Albert
1876
Proclaimed Empress of India
1887
Victoria's Golden Jubilee
1897
Victoria's Diamond Jubilee
1899
Boer War broke out
1901
Died 22nd January at Osborne House, Isle of Wight

Elizabeth II

Elizabeth II was born in 1926, the elder daughter of the Duke of York, second son of King George V, and his wife, formerly Lady Elizabeth Bowes-Lyon, daughter of the Earl of Strathmore. In 1936 George V died and Elizabeth's uncle, Edward VIII, became king. Within a year Edward abdicated and the Duke of York became King George VI.

World War II broke out in 1939 when Elizabeth was 13 years old. She and her sister Margaret spent a large part of the war at Windsor, though the King and Queen were mostly in London. Towards the end of the war Elizabeth spent some months training in the Auxiliary Territorial Service (ATS), forerunner of today's Women's Royal Army Corps, and received a commission as a junior officer.

On her 21st birthday in 1947 Elizabeth promised in a radio broadcast to the people of Britain: 'My

Scenes from the life of Elizabeth II

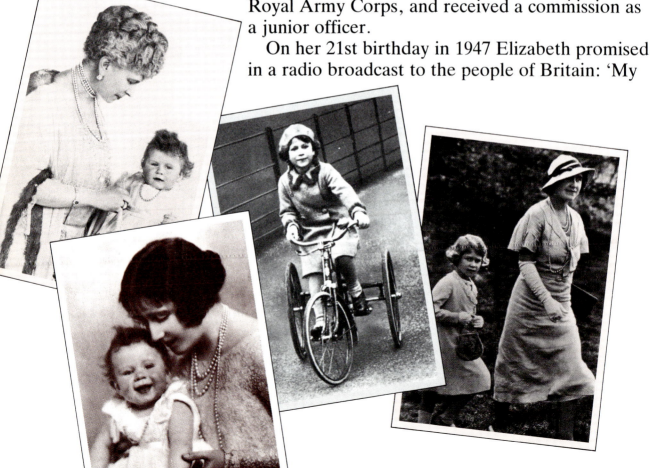

whole life…shall be devoted to your service, and to the service of our great imperial family.'

The same year she married a distant cousin, Lieutenant Philip Mountbatten of the Royal Navy. Of Danish descent, he had been Prince Philip of Greece, but was brought up in England. Philip was given the title of Duke of Edinburgh. They have four children - Charles, Anne, Andrew and Edward.

In 1948 George VI's health began to fail, and Elizabeth and her husband undertook many royal tours on his behalf. They were in Kenya on one of these tours when the King died and Elizabeth became Queen.

As Queen, Elizabeth's duties are to act as head of state, and the country is governed in her name. She takes no active part in the administration, other than signing Bills passed by Parliament to make them law.

1926
Born 21st April at 17 Bruton Street, London
1945
Served in the ATS
1947
Married Lt Philip Mountbatten, RN
1952
Became Queen
1953
Crowned in Westminster Abbey
1977
Celebrated her Silver Jubilee as Queen

36 When they ruled

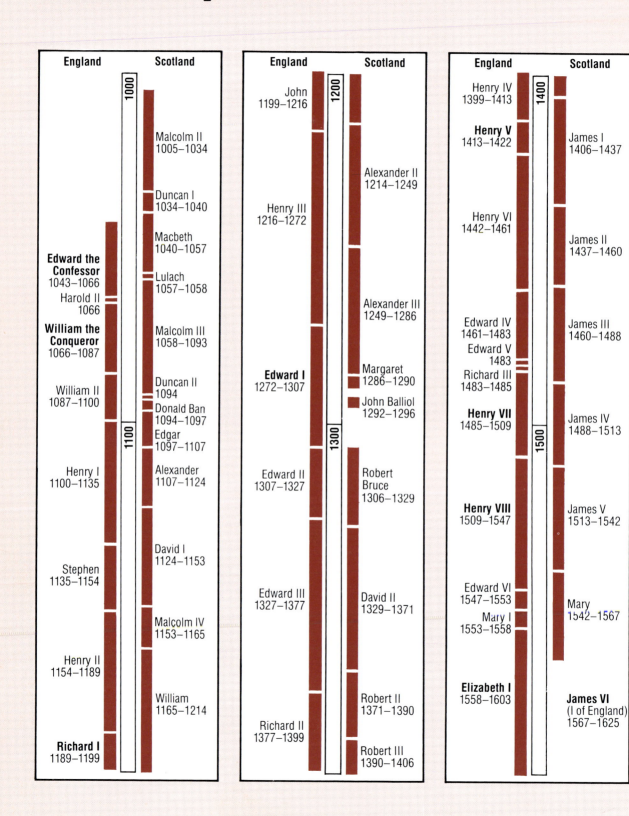

Panel 1

England | **Scotland**

1000

Malcolm II
1005–1034

Duncan I
1034–1040

Macbeth
1040–1057

Edward the Confessor
1043–1066

Lulach
1057–1058

Harold II
1066

William the Conqueror
1066–1087

Malcolm III
1058–1093

William II
1087–1100

Duncan II
1094

Donald Ban
1094–1097

Edgar
1097–1107

1100

Henry I
1100–1135

Alexander
1107–1124

David I
1124–1153

Stephen
1135–1154

Malcolm IV
1153–1165

Henry II
1154–1189

William
1165–1214

Richard I
1189–1199

Panel 2

England | **Scotland**

1200

John
1199–1216

Alexander II
1214–1249

Henry III
1216–1272

Alexander III
1249–1286

Margaret
1286–1290

Edward I
1272–1307

John Balliol
1292–1296

1300

Edward II
1307–1327

Robert Bruce
1306–1329

Edward III
1327–1377

David II
1329–1371

Robert II
1371–1390

Richard II
1377–1399

Robert III
1390–1406

Panel 3

England | **Scotland**

1400

Henry IV
1399–1413

Henry V
1413–1422

James I
1406–1437

Henry VI
1442–1461

James II
1437–1460

Edward IV
1461–1483

James III
1460–1488

Edward V
1483

Richard III
1483–1485

Henry VII
1485–1509

James IV
1488–1513

1500

Henry VIII
1509–1547

James V
1513–1542

Edward VI
1547–1553

Mary I
1553–1558

Mary
1542–1567

Elizabeth I
1558–1603

James VI
(I of England)
1567–1625

37

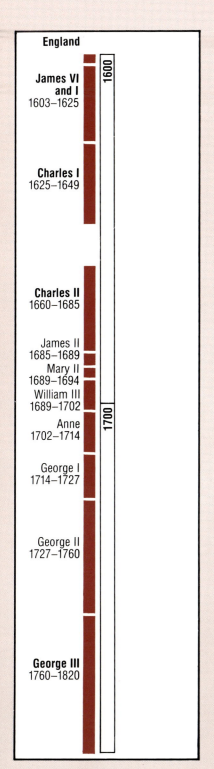

England

James VI and I 1603–1625

1600

Charles I 1625–1649

Charles II 1660–1685

James II 1685–1689
Mary II 1689–1694
William III 1689–1702
Anne 1702–1714

George I 1714–1727

1700

George II 1727–1760

George III 1760–1820

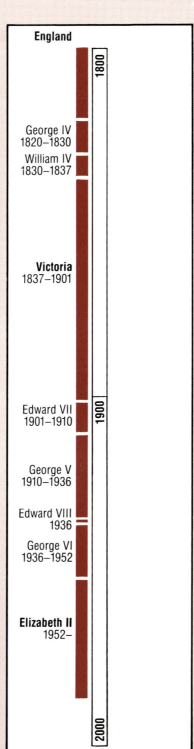

England

1800

George IV 1820–1830
William IV 1830–1837

Victoria 1837–1901

Edward VII 1901–1910

1900

George V 1910–1936

Edward VIII 1936

George VI 1936–1952

Elizabeth II 1952–

2000

The Order of Succession to the Crown

1 H.R.H. Prince of Wales
2 H.R.H. Prince William of Wales
3 H.R.H. Prince Henry of Wales
4 H.R.H. Prince Andrew
5 H.R.H. Prince Edward
6 H.R.H. Princess Anne, Mrs. Mark Phillips
7 Master Peter Phillips
8 Miss Zara Phillips
9 H.R.H. Princess Margaret, Countess of Snowdon
10 Viscount Linley
11 Lady Sarah Armstrong-Jones
12 H.R.H. Duke of Gloucester
13 Earl of Ulster
14 Lady Davina Windsor
15 Lady Rose Windsor
16 H.R.H. Duke of Kent
17 Earl of St. Andrews
18 Lord Nicholas Windsor
19 Lady Helen Windsor
20 Lord Frederick Windsor
21 Lady Gabriella Windsor
22 H.R.H. Princess Alexandra, Hon. Mrs. Angus Ogilvy
23 Mr. James Ogilvy
24 Miss Marina Ogilvy

Royal England

1 The Tower of London
2 Buckingham Palace
3 St. James's Palace
4 Marlborough House
5 Clarence House
6 Kensington Palace
7 Greenwich
8 Kew Palace
9 Hampton Court
10 Windsor Castle
11 Hatfield House
12 Sandringham House
13 Osborne House
14 Caernarvon Castle
15 Edinburgh Castle
16 Holyroodhouse
17 Balmoral

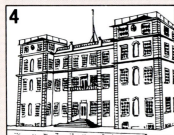

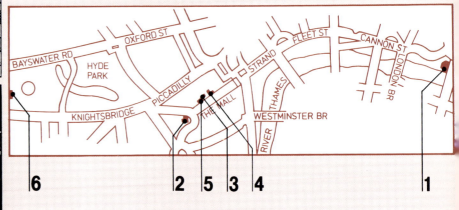

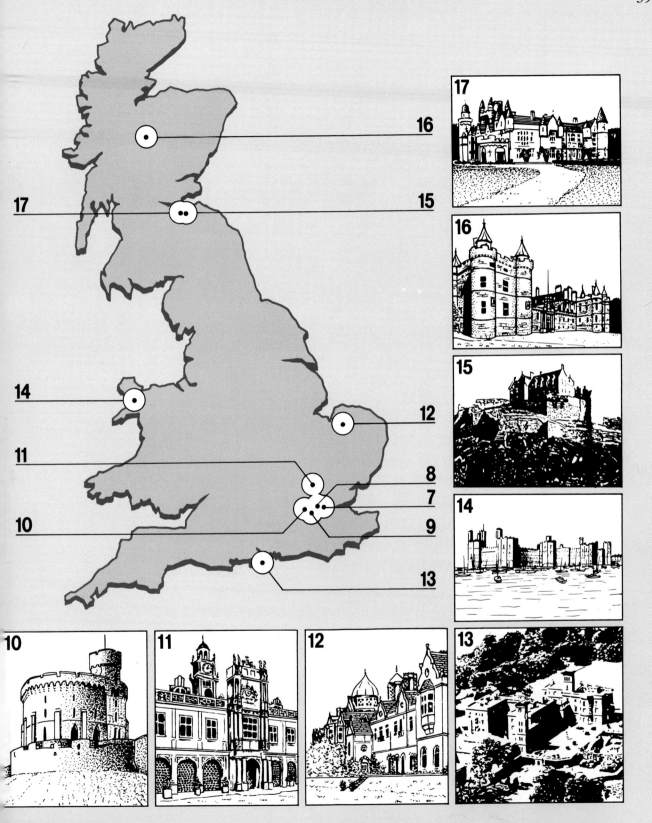

The Royal Family

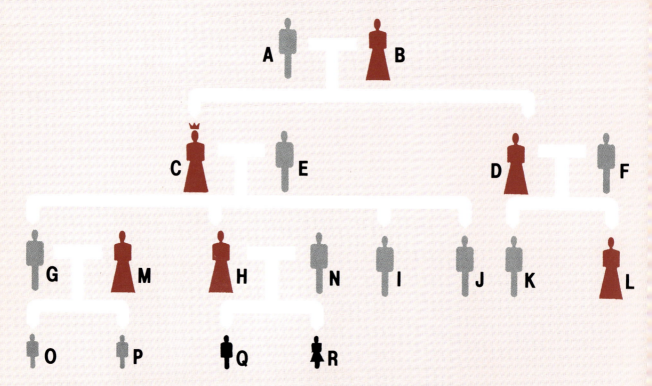

A HM King George VI (Albert Frederick Arthur George of Windsor)
B HM Queen Elizabeth the Queen Mother (Elizabeth Angela Marguerite)
C HM The Queen Elizabeth II (Elizabeth Alexandra Mary of Windsor)
D HRH The Princess Margaret (Margaret Rose, Countess of Snowdon)
E HRH The Prince Philip (Duke of Edinburgh)
F Lord Snowdon (Anthony Charles Robert Armstrong-Jones)
G HRH The Prince of Wales (Charles Philip Arthur George)
H HRH Princess Anne (Anne Elizabeth Alice Louise, Mrs Mark Philips)
I HRH Prince Andrew (Andrew Albert Christian Edward)
J HRH Prince Edward (Edward Anthony Richard Louis)
K Viscount David Linley (David Albert Charles)
L Lady Sarah Armstrong-Jones (Sarah Frances Elizabeth)
M HRH The Princess of Wales (Diana Frances)
N Captain Mark Philips (Mark Anthony Peter)
O HRH Prince William of Wales (William Arthur Philip Louis)
P HRH Prince Henry of Wales (Henry Charles Albert David)
Q Master Peter Philips (Peter Mark Andrew)
R Miss Zara Philips (Zara Anne Elizabeth)

Index

SCIENTISTS

BACON

BOYLE

NEWTON

HALLEY

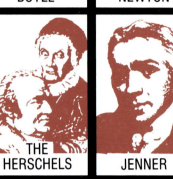

THE HERSCHELS

JENNER

DALTON

FARADAY

DARWIN

KELVIN

LISTER

MAXWELL

THOMSON

FLEMING

CRICK

EXPLORERS

FROBISHER

HUDSON

COOK

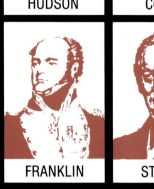

PARK

FRANKLIN

STURT

ROSS

LIVINGSTONE

SPEKE

STANLEY

YOUNGHUSBAND

SCOTT

SHACKLETON

FUCHS

FIENNES